CAREGIVING SIMPLIFIED

NAVIGATING THE MEDICAL INSURANCE MAZE

BEST HEALTHCARE PRODUCT REFERENCE GUIDE

AUTHOR: LAURIN GREY

DEDICATION

TO MY WONDERFUL PARENTS WHO I LOVE AND MISS EVERYDAY,

AND TO MY HUSBAND, THANK YOU FOR YOUR LOVE AND SUPPORT.

INTRODUCTION

CAREGIVING FOR A LOVED ONE CAN BE AN EXTRAORDINARY EXPERIENCE. IT CAN BE REWARDING AND CAN ENRICH YOUR LIFE BY TEACHING YOU LOVE, PATIENCE AND COMPASSION.

THIS QUICK REFERENCE CAREGIVING GUIDE WILL HELP SAVE YOU TIME AND MAKE YOUR CAREGIVING EXPERIENCE EASIER AND LESS STRESSFUL.

THIS BOOK WILL ALSO HELP YOU NAVIGATE THROUGH THE MEDICAL INSURANCE MAZE.

WITH 35 YEARS EXPERIENCE IN MEDICAL BILLING, I WILL EXPLAIN IN SIMPLE TERMS, THE CHOICES AVAILABLE, AND OUTLINE EACH PLAN, HELPING YOU UNDERSTAND, AND MAKE INFORMED DECISIONS REGARDING YOUR HEATHCARE.

THIS BOOK HAS BEEN WRITTEN AND PUBLISHED STRICTLY FOR INFORMATIONAL PURPOSES, AND IN NO WAY SHOULD BE USED AS A SUBSTITUTE FOR CONSULTATION WITH HEALTHCARE PROFESSIONALS. THE AUTHOR URGES ALL READERS TO BE AWARE OF THEIR HEALTH STATUS AND TO CONSULT WITH A HEALTHCARE PROFESSIONAL WHEN PROVIDING CARE AND PURCHASING MEDICAL EQUIPMENT.

ISBN 978-0-557-73659-1

CHAPTERS

CHAPTER ONE

FINDING THE BEST HEALTHCARE

MOST INSURANCE PLANS REQUIRE A PRIMARY CARE PHYSICIAN TO BE IN CHARGE OF YOUR OVERALL HEALTHCARE, AND BE RESPONSIBLE FOR REFERRING YOU TO SPECIALISTS AS NEEDED. A PRIMARY CARE PHYSICIAN SPECIALIZES IN INTERNAL MEDICINE OR FAMILY PRACTICE.

CHOOSING A PHYSICIAN IS A PERSONAL CHOICE. YOU MUST FEEL COMFORTABLE DISCUSSING PERSONAL ISSUES, AS WELL AS BE CONFIDENT IN DECISIONS YOUR DOCTOR WILL MAKE REGARDING YOUR CARE.

CHECK THE INTERNET FOR PHYSICIANS EDUCATION AND QUALIFICATIONS. YOU CAN ALSO CALL THE PHYSICIANS OFFICE, TO ASK WHICH HOSPITALS THEY ARE AFFILIATED WITH.THE AMERICAN MEDICAL ASSOCIATION AND HEALTH GRADES WEBSITES ARE AVAILABLE FOR ADDITIONAL INFORMATION:

www.ama.assn.org
www.HealthGrades.com

CHECK YOUR INSURANCE PLAN TO BE SURE THE PHYSICIAN YOU CHOOSE, IS PARTICIPATING WITH YOUR PLAN, TO ENSURE MAXIMUM COVERAGE AND BENEFITS.

PHYSICIAN PARTICIPATION IN A PLAN, IS WHEN THE DOCTOR HAS SIGNED A CONTRACT WITH THE INSURANCE COMPANY, AGREEING TO A FEE SCHEDULE, AND HE WILL WRITE OFF THE CONTRACTUAL DIFFERENCE BETWEEN HIS TOTAL CHARGES, AND WHAT THE INSURANCE COMPANY FEE SCHEDULE AGREES TO PAY, REDUCING YOUR OUT OF POCKET EXPENSES WHEN THE CLAIM IS PROCESSED.

IF THE PHYSICIAN YOU CHOOSE DOES NOT PARTICIPATE WITH YOUR INSURANCE PLAN, HE IS CONSIDERED OUT OF NETWORK, AND DEPENDING ON YOUR COVERAGE, YOUR BENEFITS COULD BE REDUCED, YOU MAY PAY MORE OUT OF POCKET, OR SERVICES MAY NOT BE COVERED AT ALL.

CONTACT YOUR INSURANCE COMPANY FOR A BENEFIT BOOKLET. THIS INFORMATION WILL EXPLAIN PLAN COVERAGE AND REIMBURSEMENT GUIDELINES. ALSO REQUEST A PARTICIPATING PROVIDER LISTING, TO ENSURE YOU ARE USING IN NETWORK PHYSICIANS.

MOST INSURANCE PLANS WILL HAVE MAXIMUM LIFETIME BENEFIT LIMIT, ANNUAL DEDUCTIBLE, COINSURANCE, AND COPAYS.

BE SURE TO COMPARE INSURANCE PLANS BEFORE CHOOSING ONE, TO ENSURE MAXIMUM COVERAGE AND BENEFITS.

CHAPTER TWO

UNDERSTANDNG INSURANCE PLANS

THERE ARE SEVERAL DIFFERENT HEALTH INSURANCE PLANS AVAILABLE:

PPO (PHYSICIAN PARTICIPATING ORGANIZATION) PATIENTS CAN SEE IN AND OUT OF NETWORK PHYSICIANS. IF PHYSICIAN IS OUT OF NETWORK, BENEFITS ARE USUALLY REDUCED, COPAYS WILL BE HIGHER AND A DEDUCTIBLE MAY HAVE TO BE MET, BEFORE BENEFITS ARE PAID.

EPO (EMPLOYER PARTICIPATING ORGANIZATION) SELF FUNDED PLANS (EMPLOYER PAYS CLAIMS). ONLY IN NETWORK BENEFITS, MUST USE IN NETWORK PHYSICIANS AND FACILITIES FOR COVERAGE.

INDEMNITY (PRIVATE PLAN PURCHASED BY AN INDIVIDUAL) USUALLY HAVE DEDUCTIBLES AND COINSURANCE.

HMO INSURANCE HAS ONLY IN NETWORK BENEFITS AND YOU CAN ONLY USE PARTICIPATING PHYSICIANS AND FACILITIES FOR COVERAGE.

PFFS PROVIDER FEE FOR SERVICE PLANS ARE INSURANCE PLANS WITH COPAYS AND LIMITATIONS AND REQUIRE PHYSICIAN PARTICIPATION.

MEDICARE PART A AND B   ELIGIBLE INDIVIDUALS MUST BE DISABLED OR AGE 65 TO QUALIFY FOR THIS INSURANCE COVERAGE. MEDICARE WILL PAY 80% ACCORDING TO MEDICARE'S FEE SCHEDULE, AND YOU WOULD BE RESPONSIBLE FOR A 20% BALANCE.

IF THE PHYSICIAN IS PARTICIPATING WITH MEDICARE, HE AGREES TO CHARGE ONLY THE FEE APPROVED BY MEDICARE, AND WILL WRITE OFF THE DIFFERENCE BETWEEN THE AMOUNT CHARGED, AND THE 80% ALLOWED AMOUNT ACCORDING TO THE MEDICARE FEE SCHEDULE. PATIENT WILL BE RESPONSIBLE FOR 20% OF THE MEDICARE APPROVED AMOUNT. A PARTICIPATING PHYSICIAN WILL ALSO FILE YOUR SECONDARY INSURANCE, TO COLLECT THE 20% AFTER MEDICARE HAS PAID.

IF THE PHYSICIAN IS NON PARTICIPATING WITH MEDICARE, THEY CAN CHARGE YOU THEIR TOTAL FEE UPFRONT, AND THEY WILL SUBMIT YOUR CLAIM TO MEDICARE FOR YOUR REIMBURSEMENT. YOU WOULD NEED TO WAIT TO RECEIVE THE EXPLANATION OF BENEFITS FROM MEDICARE, TO FILE TO YOUR SECONDARY PLAN, TO REIMBURSE YOU FOR THE 20% COINSURANCE. YOU WOULD NOT BE REIMBURSED THE DIFFERENCE BETWEEN THE TOTAL FEE AND THE MEDICARE FEE SCHEDULE.

CHAPTER THREE

INSURANCE COVERAGE FOR SENIORS AND THE DISABLED

MEDICARE IS A FEDERAL INSURANCE PLAN FOR INDIVIDUALS WHO QUALIFY BY BEING OVER 65 YEARS OLD, DISABLED, OR HAVE END STAGE RENAL DISEASE.

A PERSON IS AUTOMATICALLY ELIGIBLE FOR MEDICARE PART A IF THEY HAVE WORKED FOR 10 YEARS, OR FOR AT LEAST 40 QUARTERS DURING A LIFETIME. THIS ACCRUED TIME DOES NOT HAVE TO BE CONSECUTIVE. IF THESE REQUIREMENTS ARE NOT MET, AN INDIVIDUAL CAN CHOOSE TO PAY FOR THIS COVERAGE.

SENIORS AND DISABLED INDIVIDUALS WILL HAVE THE CHOICE TO ADD MEDICARE PART B COVERAGE, MEDICARE PART D (PRESCRIPTION DRUG COVERAGE), SUPPLIMENTAL PRIVATE PLANS OR CHOOSE MEDICARE HMO PLANS. MEDICARE HMO PLANS TAKE THE PLACE OF TRADITIONAL MEDICARE AND SUPPLIMENTAL PLANS.

MEDICARE PART A COVERS HOSPITAL SERVICES, WHICH INCLUDES THE FACILITY CHARGES, ANESTHESIA, OPERATING ROOM CHARGES, DRUGS USED WHILE HOSPITALIZED, AMBULANCE, AND DURABLE MEDICAL EQUIPMENT.

MEDICARE PART A HAS A DEDUCTIBLE FOR EACH INPATIENT HOSPITAL STAY. WHEN ADMITTED TO THE HOSPITAL AS OBSERVATION STATUS, OR FOR UNDER 24 HOURS, THIS ADMISSION IS CONSIDERED OUTPATIENT, AND IS NOT SUBJECT TO THE INPATIENT DEDUCTIBLE.

MEDICARE PART A ALSO OFFERS HOSPICE MEDICAL COVERAGE FOR THE TERMINALLY ILL. THIS COVERAGE INCLUDES CAREGIVING SUPPORT FOR THE PATIENT AND THEIR FAMILY MEMBERS.

MEDICARE PART B IS ELECTIVE ADDITIONAL COVERAGE, AND HAS A MONTHLY PREMIUM. PLAN B IS FOR PHYSICIAN SERVICES, SUCH AS DOCTOR OFFICE CHARGES, RADIOLOGY AND LAB IN AN OUTPATIENT SETTING. THERE IS AN ANNUAL DEDUCTIBLE THAT MUST BE MET, BEFORE BENEFITS ARE PAID.

MEDICARE SUPPLIMENTAL PLANS ARE AVAILABLE BY PAYING MONTHLY PREMIUMS SUCH AS: AARP, BANKERS LIFE, UNITED AMERICAN, BLUE CROSS BLUE SHIELD, ETC. THEY COVER THE 20% COINSURANCE AFTER MEDICARE PAYS, AND SOME PLANS WILL ALSO COVER THE ANNUAL MEDICARE DEDUCTIBLES AND OFFER PRESCRIPTION DRUG COVERAGE.

THESE PLANS ARE ALSO CALLED "MEDIGAP" PLANS, BECAUSE THEY AUTOMATICALLY GET FILED BY MEDICARE, TO PICK UP THE 20% COINSURANCE, WITHOUT HAVING TO SEND A PAPER CLAIM FOR PROCESSING.

THE THREE MOST POPULAR MEDIGAP PLANS ARE:

AARP

www.aarp.org (888) 687-2277

AARP ALSO OFFERS A MEMBERSHIP FOR INDIVIDUALS AGE FIFTY AND OLDER, WHICH INCLUDES A MONTHLY NEWSLETTER AND DISCOUNTS. THIS MEMBERSHIP DOES HAVE AN ANNUAL FEE.

BANKERS LIFE AND CASUALTY INSURANCE COMPANY

www.bankers.com (800) 231-9150

UNITED AMERICAN INSURANCE

www.unitedamerican.com (972) 529-5085

BLUE CROSS BLUE SHIELD OFFERS MEDICARE MEDIGAP SUPPLIMENTAL PLANS. YOU CAN CONTACT YOUR LOCAL STATE BLUE CROSS BLUE SHIELD PLAN FOR ADDITIONAL INFORMATION.

MEDICAID IS MEDICAL ASSISTANCE INSURANCE FOR PEOPLE WHO ARE DISABLED OR CANNOT AFFORD MEDICAL BILLS OR INSURANCE, DUE TO LOW INCOME, END STAGE RENAL DISEASE OR PERMANENT DISABILITY. THE DEPARTMENT OF SOCIAL SERVICES WITHIN YOUR STATE AND COUNTY CAN CHECK TO SEE IF YOU QUALIFY FOR THIS MEDICAL COVERAGE.

MEDICARE PART D IS OUTPATIENT PRESCRIPTION DRUG COVERAGE, WHICH CAN BE PURCHASED BY PAYING AN ADDITIONAL MONTHLY PREMIUM. THIS COVERAGE HAS LIMITATIONS AND COPAYS.

MEDICARE ADVANTAGE PLANS, TAKE THE PLACE OF MEDICARE, COST LESS OUT OF POCKET, AND ARE ACTUALLY AN HMO POLICY, WITH RESTRICTION GUIDELINES, DEDUCTIBLES, AND COPAYS.

THESE MEDICARE HMO PLANS OFFER A LOWER DEDUCTIBLE THAN THE TRADITIONAL MEDICARE PLAN, AND COPAYS MUST BE PAID FOR OUTPATIENT SERVICES AND HOSPITALIZATIONS.

SOME PLANS REQUIRE YOU TO USE PARTICIPATING PHYSICIANS AND FACILITIES. MEDICARE HMO INSURANCE PLAN EXAMPLES ARE: BLUE MEDICARE, HUMANA GOLD CHOICE PLAN, SECURE HORIZONS, BLUE MEDICARE, ETC

WHEN CHOOSING A MEDICARE HMO, BE CAREFUL TO CHECK:

1. INDIVIDUAL COPAYS FOR EXPENSIVE MRI AND CAT SCAN TESTS
2. YOUR PHYSICIAN AND HOSPITAL ARE PARTICIPATING
3. HOSPITAL ADMISSION, OBSERVATION, EMERGENCY ROOM COPAYS
4. MAXIMUM LIFETIME BENEFIT LIMITS

MEDICARE HMO PLANS WILL DIFFER BY CHARGING A DAILY HOSPITAL ADMISSION COPAY, OR A SINGLE COPAY FOR THE ENTIRE HOSPITAL STAY.

BEWARE OF HIGH COPAYS FOR RADIOLOGY SCANS SUCH AS MRI OR CAT SCANS. THESE COPAYS CAN ADD UP QUICKLY WHEN BEING DIAGNOSED FOR STROKE OR CANCER.

CHECK YOUR PLAN LIMITS FOR THE MAXIMUM BENEFITS AVAILABLE FOR YOUR LIFETIME

MOST COMMON MEDICARE HMO PLANS:

BLUE MEDICARE (FORMERLY BC PARTNERS)	(888) 310-4110
HUMANA GOLD CHOICE	(800) 523-0023
SECURE HORIZONS (UNITED HEALTHCARE)	(800) 638-3323

YOU CAN ALSO CHECK THE INTERNET FOR INFORMATION ON THESE INDIVIDUAL PLANS.

INSURANCE PLANS WILL COVER WELLNESS SCREENINGS FOR COLON CANCER (COLONOSCOPY), BREAST CANCER (MAMMOGRAPHY), GLAUCOMA, WHICH CAN CAUSE BLINDNESS, PAP SMEARS, TO SCREEN FOR CERVICAL CANCER AND BONE DENSITY SCANS TO RULE OUT OSTEOPOROSIS.

THESE SCREENINGS ARE VERY IMPORTANT FOR YOUR OVERALL HEALTH. SPEAK TO YOUR PHYSICIAN REGARDING THESE TESTS, AND CHECK YOUR INSURANCE PLAN FOR COVERAGE AND IF PRECERTIFICATION IS NEEDED.

ALL PRIMARY INSURANCE PLANS, MEDICARE HMO PLANS AND SECONDARY INSURANCE TO MEDICARE, REQUIRE NOTIFICATION WHEN ADMITTED TO A HOSPITAL. MEDICARE DOES NOT REQUIRE NOTIFICATION. HOSPITALS WILL NOTIFY YOUR INSURANCE COMPANY. THIS AUTHORIZATION INSURES THE CLAIM WILL BE PAID.

MOST OUTPATIENT PROCEDURES ALSO REQUIRE PRECERTIFICATION AND ARE USUALLY HANDLED BY YOUR PHYSICIANS BILLING DEPARTMENT WHEN SCHEDULED. ALL PATIENTS SHOULD FOLLOW UP TO MAKE SURE THESE REQUIREMENTS HAVE BEEN MET, AND TO INSURE THE SERVICE IS COVERED AND WILL BE PAID.

CHAPTER FOUR

HOSPITALIZATION- HOME HEALTH VS NURSING HOME

WHEN YOU ARE ADMITTED TO A HOSPITAL, YOU WILL HAVE CHOICES TO MAKE REGARDING YOUR OVERALL CARE. DISCUSS YOUR WISHES WITH YOUR PHYSICIAN. IF A LOVED ONE IS HOSPITALIZED, YOU MAY WANT TO CONSIDER STAYING OVERNIGHT WITH THEM, TO INSURE PROPER CARE. MOST HOSPITALS WILL ACCOMMODATE THIS REQUEST.

WHEN CALLING AN AMBULANCE FOR TRANSPORT TO A HOSPITAL, MAKE SURE YOUR PHYSICAN HAS PRIVLEDGES AT THE FACILITY. IF YOUR PHYSICIAN DOES NOT HAVE PRVILEDGES AT THE CLOSEST HOSPITAL, A HOSPITALIST WILL BE ASSIGNED TO CARE FOR YOU, AND HE WILL COMMUNICATE WITH YOUR PRIMARY CARE DOCTOR, TO COORDINATE CARE.

SOME INJURIES AND ILLNESSES MAY REQUIRE PHYSICAL, SPEECH, OR OCCUPATIONAL THERAPY. THESE SERVICES CAN BE OFFERED IN A NURSING HOME, REHABILITATION CENTER, OR YOU MAY CHOOSE TO RECEIVE HOME CARE, IN THE PRIVACY OF YOUR OWN HOME.

IF YOU ARE REFERRED TO A NURSING HOME BY YOUR PHYSICIAN, YOU CAN USE THE INTERNET WEBSITE www.medicare.gov/Nursing/Overview.asp TO CHECK NURSING HOME RATINGS NATIONWIDE.

THIS WEBSITE WILL HELP YOU MAKE EDUCATED CHOICES, AND INSURE THE BEST FACILITY, FOR YOUR RECUPERATON.

ALSO BE SURE TO CONTACT THE FACILITY DIRECTLY, TO MAKE SURE THEY PARTICIPATE WITH YOUR INSURANCE PLAN.

ALSO CHECK THESE WEBSITES FOR FREE INFORMATON

www.carepathways.com.

www.eldercarelink.com

IF YOU CHOOSE TO RECUPERATE AT HOME, HOME HEALTH CARE CAN BE ORDERED BY YOUR PHYSICIAN, AND MAY BE COVERED BY MEDICARE FOR A PERIOD OF TIME. NURSES CAN PROVIDE DAILY MEDICAL CARE WITH MEDICATION MANAGEMENT, AND NURSING AIDES CAN PROVIDE CUSTODIAL CARE, SUCH AS BATHING AND PERSONAL HYGIENE.

FAMILY MEMBERS CAN ALSO PARTICIPATE IN YOUR CARE THROUGH TRAINING FROM THESE NURSING PROFESSIONALS. THERAPISTS CAN SHOW FAMILY MEMBERS HOW TO CONTINUE THE THERAPY WHILE AT HOME, TO SPEED UP RECOVERY TIME.

AN OCCUPATIONAL THERAPIST WILL EVALUATE YOUR HOME WHEN YOU ARE DISCHARGED FROM THE HOSPITAL, AND OFFER RECOMMENDATIONS TO ADD SAFETY EQUIPMENT SUCH AS GRAB BARS, AND BEDSIDE COMMODES, WHICH WILL MAKE DAILY ACTIVITIES EASIER AND SAFER.

IN CASES OF STAPH INFECTIONS, PATIENTS CAN REQUEST TO RECEIVE ANTIBIOTIC THERAPY AT HOME, INSTEAD OF BEING HOSPITALIZED OR SENT TO A REHABILITATION CENTER FOR TREATMENT. A PATIENT CAN RECEIVE THIS THERAPY AT HOME WITH NURSING HOME CARE SUPPORT AND TRAINING FOR FAMILY MEMBERS.

YOUR PHYSICIAN WILL HAVE TO WRITE AN ORDER FOR YOU TO RECEIVE THIS CARE AT HOME.

YOUR PHYSICIAN CAN ALSO ORDER DURABLE MEDICAL EQUIPMENT SUCH AS BEDSIDE COMMODES, WALKERS, OR WHEELCHAIRS.

MEDICARE WILL COVER THE COST OF A SCOOTER OR ELECTRIC WHEELCHAIR ONCE IN A LIFETIME, FOR CERTAIN MEDICAL CONDITIONS. PROPER DIAGNOSIS IS REQUIRED FOR COVERAGE.

ALL HOSPITALS HAVE A DISCHARGE PLANNING DEPARTMENT WHICH CAN HELP COORDINATE, AND SET UP THESE SERVICES BEFORE YOU ARE DISCHARGED TO INSURE THE CONTINUATION OF PROPER CARE.

CHAPTER FIVE

PERSONAL HEALTH CARE DECISIONS AND DOCUMENTS

A POWER OF ATTORNEY IS A LEGAL DOCUMENT WHICH COMMUNICATES YOUR WISHES, IN CASE YOU ARE NOT ABLE TO COMMUNICATE ON YOUR OWN. THIS DOCUMENT COVERS FINANCIAL, REAL ESTATE AND MEDICAL ISSUES. YOU CAN APPOINT A FAMILY MEMBER OR FRIEND, TO MAKE THESE DECISIONS FOR YOU.

A LIVING WILL IS A DOCUMENT THAT COMMUNICATES YOUR WISHES REGARDING YOUR MEDICAL CARE. IT COMMUNICATES WHETHER OR NOT YOU WANT TO BE RESUSCITATED IN CASE OF CARDIAC ARREST, OR TO BE PLACED ON MACHINES TO PROLONG YOUR LIFE. A DNR FORM IS A "DO NOT RESUSCITATE" DOCUMENT WHICH CAN BE PLACED IN YOUR MEDICAL RECORD AND FAMILY MEMBERS CAN KEEP A COPY, IN CASE OF AN EMERGENCY.

YOU MAY ALSO CHOOSE TO EXPRESS YOUR WISHES TO YOUR FAMILY MEMBERS AND LEAVE THESE DECISIONS UP TO THEM TO DECIDE, IF AND WHEN THE SITUATION ARISES.

THESE FORMS CAN BE COMPLETED ON YOUR OWN, BY AN ATTORNEY, OR WITH HELP FROM A FAMILY MEMBER, AND MUST BE NOTARIZED BY A NOTARY.

AN ATTORNEY IS NOT REQUIRED FOR THESE DOCUMENTS TO BE LEGAL.

THESE FORMS ARE AVAILABLE ON THE INTERNET, AT ANY HOSPITAL OR BOOK STORE, AND REQUIRE A NOTARY TO ATTEST TO YOUR SIGNATURE. EVERY STATE HAS THEIR OWN LEGAL REQUIREMENTS AND THEREFORE FORMS SHOULD BE COMPLETED IN THE STATE WHERE YOU RESIDE.

CHAPTER SIX

TOLL FREE NUMBERS OF INTEREST FOR CAREGIVERS

AARP	800-424-2277
ALZHEIMER'S ASSOCIATION HEADQUARTERS	800-272-3900
AMERICAN CANCER SOCIETY	800-227-2345
ELDERCARE LOCATOR	800-677-1116
FAMILY CAREGIVERS ALLIANCE	800-445-8106
GRIEF RECOVERY HOTLINE	800-445-4808
HEARING HELPLINE (BETTER HEARING INSTITUTE)	800-327-9355
MEDICARE DURABLE MEDICAL EQUIPMENT	800-213-5452
MEDICARE FRAUD AND ABUSE HOTLINE	800-368-5779
MEDICARE HOME HEALTH HOTLINE	800-624-3004
MEDICARE TELEPHONE HOTLINE	800-638-6833
NATIONAL CANCER INSTITUTE	800-422-6237
NATIONAL COUNCIL ON AGING	800-424-9046
NATIONAL INSURANCE CONSUMER HELPLINE	800-942-4242
NATIONAL STROKE ASSOCIATION	800-787-6537
SENIORS HEALTH INSURANCE INFORMATION PROGRAM	800-443-9354
SOCIAL SECURITY ADMINISTRATION	800-772-1213
TRICARE (MILITARY HEALTHCARE)	800-363-6337

CHAPTER SEVEN

NATIONWIDE HEALTH INSURANCE INFORMATION FOR CAREGIVERS

ALABAMA	800-243-5463
ALASKA	800-478-6065
COLORADO	800-696-7213
CONNECTICUT	800-994-9422
DELAWARE	800-336-9500
DISTRICT OF COLUMBIA	202-739-0668
FLORIDA	800-963-5337
GEORGIA	800-669-8387
HAWAII	888-875-9229
IDAHO	800-247-4422
ILLINOIS	800-548-9034
INDIANA	800-452-4800
IOWA	800-351-4664
KANSAS	800-860-5260
MICHIGAN	800-803-7174
MINNESOTA	800-333-2433
MISSISSIPPI	800-948-3090
MISSOURI	800-390-3330
MONTANA	406-444-4077
NEBRASKA	800-234-7119
NEVADA	800-307-4444
NEW HAMPSHIRE	866-634-9412
NEW YORK	800-701-0501
NORTH CAROLINA	800-443-9354
RHODE ISLAND	401-222-2858
SOUTH CAROLINA	803-898-2997
SOUTH DAKOTA	800-536-8197
TENNESSEE	877-801-0044
TEXAS	800-252-9240
VERMONT	800-631-7788
VIRGINIA	800-552-3402
WASHINGTON	800-562-6900
WEST VIRGINIA	877-987-4463
WISCONSIN	800-236-8517
WYOMING	800-856-4398

SENIORS HEALTH INSURANCE INFORMATION PROGRAM (SHIIP) IS A NATIONWIDE PROGRAM AVAILABLE TO ANSWER QUESTIONS AND COUNSEL MEDICARE BENEFICIARIES AND CAREGIVERS ABOUT MEDICARE, MEDICARE SUPPLIMENT PLANS, MEDICARE ADVANTAGE PLANS, MEDICARE PRESCRIPTION DRUG PLANS, LONG TERM CARE INSURANCE AND OTHER HEALTH INSURANCE BILLING CONCERNS.

SHIIP: 1-800-443-9354.

THE NATIONAL ASSOCIATION OF HOME CARE OFFERS INFORMATION ON:

WHAT IS HOME CARE
WHO PROVIDES CARE
WHAT TYPE OF SERVICES ARE PROVIDED
WHO PAYS FOR THESE SERVICES
BILLING PRACTICES
SELECTING A HOME CARE AGENCY
PATIENT RIGHTS
ACCREDITING AGENCIES

MEDICARE OFFERS A SERVICE CALLED "HOME HEALTH COMPARE". THIS SERVICE OFFERS DETAILED INFORMATION ABOUT MEDICARE CERTIFIED HOME HEALTH AGENCIES. SEARCHES CAN BE DONE BY ZIP CODE, STATE OR AGENCY NAME.

MEDICARE INFORMATION IS AVAILABLE ON THE INTERNET AT:

www.medicare.gov

BEST PRODUCT REFERENCE GUIDE

1. **HANDICAP EQUIPMENT RESOURCES**

   HANDICAP PRECAUTIONS TO PREVENT FALLS

   BED GUARDS

   WALKERS VS WHEELCHAIRS

   ELECTRIC SCOOTERS VS ELECTRIC WHEELCHAIRS

   HANDICAP EQUIPMENT FOR THE HOME

   EASY HANDICAP DOOR MODIFICATIONS

2. **HANDICAP TRANSPORTATION/ PUBLIC VS PRIVATE**

   HANDICAP ACCESSABLE VANS/TAS SYSTEM

   ELECTRIC VS PORTABLE RAMPS

3. **ITEMS TO ASSIST SENIORS CONTINUE THEIR INDEPENDENT LIVING**

   ALARM SYSTEMS WITH VOICE COMMUNICATION

   LIFECALL-MEDICAL MONITORING SYSTEMS

   MEALS ON WHEELS

4. **PERSONAL HEALTH PRODUCTS**

WOUND CARE:

EASY PAIN FREE LIFTING AND TRANSFERRING

INCONTINENCE PRODUCTS FOR ADULTS

BEST HEMORRHOID CREAM

PAIN RELIEF

5. **SKIN CARE**

SKIN MOISTURIZING

PRODUCTS TO PREVENT BED SORES

6. **PERSONAL BATHING**

BATH CHAIRS AND SLIDING BENCHES FOR EASY BATH TUB ACCESS

7. **BED BOUND CARE**

INFLATABLE HAIR SHAMPOO TUBS

INFLATABLE FULL SIZE BATH TUB

8. **MEDICATIONS**

THE PDR POCKET GUIDE TO PRESCRIPTION DRUGS

DAILY MEDICATION LIST

AUTOMATIC PRESCRIPTION RENEWAL

9. **NUTRITIONAL SUPPLIMENTS**

STAYING HEALTHY AND EATING RIGHT

OVER THE COUNTER VITAMINS

NUTRITIONAL DRINKS

10. **AVOIDING INFECTIONS/TAKING PRECAUTIONS**

HAND WASHING

PROTECTIVE GLOVES

DISINFECTING WIPES

HANDICAP SAFETY EQUIPMENT

SAFETY AT HOME SHOULD BE A PRIORITY. EASY MODIFICATIONS AND PRECAUTIONS CAN PREVENT INJURIES AND DISABILITIES.

ALWAYS USE RUBBER BACKED RUGS TO PREVENT SLIPS AND FALLS.

INSTALL HANDICAP WALL GRAB HANDLES IN THE BATH FOR SAFETY. THEY ARE INEXPENSIVE AND ARE AVAILABLE AT YOUR LOCAL MEDICAL SUPPLY, HOME IMPROVEMENT STORE OR ON THE INTERNET.

TO WIDEN DOORWAYS TO ACCOMMODATE A WHEELCHAIR OR SCOOTER YOU CAN CHANGE THE STANDARD DOOR HINGES TO OFFSET HINGES WHICH WILL ADD TWO INCHES TO ANY DOOR WAY WITHOUT EXPENSIVE MODIFICATION.

OFFSET HINGES ARE AVAILABLE AT:

ADAPTIVE ACCESS.COM

ALL WAYS ACCESSABLE (800) 684-0270

TO PREVENT FALLING OUT OF BED, USE A BED GUARD. THESE GUARDS ALSO HELP YOU SIT UP EASILY, WITHOUT CAUSING BACK PAIN.
BED GUARDS CAN BE PURCHASED AT YOUR LOCAL MEDICAL SUPPLY STORE.

WALKERS, WHEELCHAIRS AND SCOOTERS ARE AVAILABLE AT MEDICAL SUPPLY STORES TO HELP WITH MOBILITY. YOUR PHYSICIAN MUST WRITE A PRESCRIPTION TO ORDER THE EQUIPMENT, AND A PROPER DIAGNOSIS MUST BE USED FOR INSURANCE COVERAGE.

LIGHT WEIGHT FOLDING ALUMINUM WHEELCHAIRS ARE AVAILABLE TO MAKE TRAVELING IN CARS AND AIRPLANES EASY. THESE WHEELCHAIRS FOLD FLAT FOR EASY STORAGE.

WALKERS ARE AVAILABLE TO ASSIST INDIVIDUALS WITH BALANCE. MEDICARE WILL ONLY COVER A STANDARD ALUMINUM WALKER, WHICH HAS NO WHEELS AND MUST BE LIFTED TO MOVE FORWARD.

THE BEST WALKERS AVAILABLE COME WITH 4 WHEELS FOR STABILITY, LOCKING HAND BRAKES, AND HAVE A SEAT FOR SITTING WITH STORAGE.

THESE UPGRADED WALKERS ALSO FOLD FLAT AND MUST BE PURCHASED OUT OF POCKET, BUT ARE WELL WORTH THE INVESTMENT FOR MOBILITY AND COMFORT.

AN ELECTRIC WHEELCHAIR IS EASIER TO MANEUVER. A SCOOTER MAY BECOME DIFFICULT TO USE AS A PERSON AGES, OR IF A SHOULDER INJURY OCCURS.

THESE UPGRADED WHEELCHAIRS, WALKERS AND SCOOTERS ARE AVAILABLE IN DIFFERENT COLORS. BE SURE TO SPECIFY THE COLOR AT THE TIME OF PURCHASE.

ASSISTIVE TECHNOLOGY

YOUR PHYSICIAN CAN ORDER ORTHODICS (WALKING COMFORT AIDS) OR PROSTHETICS (REPLACEMENT LIMBS) IF NEEDED

THIS EQUIPMENT IS CUSTOM MADE TO FIT AND INSURANCE WILL COVER WHEN A PRESCRIPTION IS WRITTEN WITH CORRECT DIAGNOSIS.

BEST MEDICAL PRODUCT CATALOG

"NORTH COAST'S FUNCTIONAL SOLUTIONS" IS A CATALOG OF THERAPIST RECOMMENDED PRODUCTS TO ASSIST WITH DAILY LIVING. YOU CAN ORDER PRODUCTS 24 HOURS A DAY SEVEN DAYS A WEEK, AND MOST PRODUCTS ARE SHIPPED THE SAME DAY FOR QUICK DELIVERY.

NORTH COAST FUNCTIONAL SOLUTIONS (800) 235-7054

www.BeAbleToDo.com

HANDICAP TRANSPORTATION

SOME CITIES AND COUNTIES OFFER SENIOR TRANSPORTATION SERVICES. SOME SERVICES HAVE A SMALL FEE AND ARE SCHEDULED BY APPOINTMENT. YOU CAN CHECK WITH YOUR LOCAL SENIOR CENTER TO SEE IF ANY SERVICES ARE AVAILABLE IN YOUR AREA.

DISABLED INDIVIDUALS CAN ALSO TRAVEL USING A PROFESSIONALLY MODIFIED VAN. USUALLY THESE HANDICAP VANS HAVE AN ELECTRIC RAMP, WHICH IS AN EXPENSIVE MODIFICATION. AN ALTERNATIVE IS TO PURCHASE A VAN, WHICH CAN EASILY ACCOMMODATE A WHEELCHAIR BY REMOVING SEATS, AND USING A PORTABLE RAMP. WHEN THE VAN IS NOT BEING USED TO TRANSPORT A WHEELCHAIR, IT CAN BE EASILY TURNED BACK INTO A FAMILY CONVERSION VAN.

AFTER YEARS OF INVESTIGATION, THE ONLY VAN I FOUND WAS AN EXPLORER HIGHTOP CONVERSION VAN WHICH OFFERS A QUICK RELEASE SEAT OPTION. WHEN THE CENTER CAPTAIN SEATS ARE REMOVED, THE FLOOR OF THE VAN IS FLUSH, ALLOWING A WHEELCHAIR OR SCOOTER TO EASILY RIDE INTO THE VEHICLE. THE HIGHTOP ROOF FEATURE ALLOWS ENOUGH HEAD ROOM TO MANEUVER AND SIT COMFORTABLY.

A 7 FOOT PORTABLE FOLDING ALUMINUM LIGHT WEIGHT RAMP CAN BE USED DURING VAN TRANSPORT, INSTEAD OF USING EXPENSIVE MOTORIZED RAMPS.

THESE FOLDING RAMPS CAN BE PURCHASED ON THE INTERNET. PRICES DO VARY, SO SHOP AROUND. THE BEST RAMP I FOUND WAS A TWO PIECE DESIGN, INTERLOCKING FOLDING SUITCASE RAMP, WHICH WAS EASY TO USE, HAD HANDLES FOR LIFTING AND WAS LIGHT WEIGHT ALUMINUM.

THE LIGHT WEIGHT TRIFOLD SUITCASE 2 PIECE RAMP CAN BE FOUND AT

SCOOTERVILLE
E Z ACCESS (800) 689-0030

A TAS SYSTEM (TURNING AUTOMOTIVE SEAT) IS AVAILABLE FOR AUTOMOTIVE TRANSPORT. THIS MOTORIZED SYSTEM ALLOWS THE FRONT SEAT IN CERTAIN VANS AND SUVS TO TURN, MOVE DOWN TO ALLOW THE PERSON TO SIT ON THE CHAIR, AND THEN LIFTS THE PERSON AND SLIDES BACK INTO THE VEHICLE. THIS MODIFICATION IS EXPENSIVE AND MUST BE PROFESSIONALY INSTALLED. FOR ADDITIONAL INFO SEE

BRUNO INDEPENDENT LIVING AIDS
www.bruno.com (800) 882-8183

EBAY IS A GREAT INTERNET SITE TO FIND MEDICAL EQUIPMENT AT LOW PRICES. MAKE SURE TO CHECK PRODUCT WARRANTIES AND REFUND POLICIES BEFORE MAKING A PURCHASE.

ITEMS TO ASSIST WITH INDEPENDENT LIVING

MOST SENIORS AND DISABLED INDIVIDUALS WANT TO KEEP LIVING INDEPENDENTLY FOR AS LONG AS POSSIBLE. YOU CAN CHECK WITH THE COUNTY WHERE YOU LIVE TO SEE WHAT PROGRAMS ARE AVAILABLE. SENIOR CENTERS OFFER MANY RESOURCES AND PROGRAMS TO ASSIST WITH DAILY LIVING.

ALARM SYSTEMS

"LIFE ALERT IS A PERSONAL SECURITY SYSTEM, WHICH HELPS INDIVIDUALS FEEL SAFE, ESPECIALLY IF LIVING AT HOME ALONE. THE SECURITY DEVICE IS WORN AROUND THE NECK AND WHEN PRESSED, CONNECTS DIRECTLY TO THE POLICE, FIRE DEPARTMENT AND 911 OPERATOR DURING AN EMERGENCY. THERE IS A MONTHLY MONITORING FEE FOR THIS SERVICE.

LIFE ALERT (800) 844-9513

HOME SECURITY SYSTEMS INSURE SAFETY AT HOME. THE BEST HOME ALARM SYSTEMS COME WITH VOICE COMMUNICATION. WHICH YOU CAN VERBALLY COMMUNICATE OVER A SPEAKER WITH SECURITY PERSONNEL DURING AN EMERGENCY. THERE IS A MONTHLY MONITORING CHARGE, BUT THE INSTALLATION AND EQUIPMENT ARE USUALLY FREE.

MEDICAL ALERT PRODUCTS

MEDICAL ALERT BRACELETS ARE AVAILABLE FOR PURCHASE AT YOUR LOCAL PHARMACY. THESE BRACELETS DISPLAY ANY MEDICAL CONDITIONS YOU MAY HAVE SUCH AS, DIABETES OR HEART PROBLEMS. MEDICAL ALERT NECKLACES ARE ALSO AVAILABLE.

IN CASE OF AN EMERGENCY **CALL 911**

MAKE SURE ALL EMERGENCY PHONE NUMBERS ARE EASILY AVAILABLE. KEEP THEM NEAR YOUR TELEPHONE OR POSTED ON YOUR REFRIGERATOR.

REMEMBER TO TAKE CARE OF YOUR PETS AND KEEP THEM SAFE. KEEP ALL MEDICATIONS AWAY FROM YOUR CHILDREN AND PETS. IN CASE OF AN EMERGENCY, CALL 911 OR CONTACT YOUR VETERINARIAN IMMEDIATELY.

LOCAL SERVICES

"MEALS ON WHEELS" IS A PROGRAM WHICH DELIVERS MEALS TO YOUR HOME DAILY FOR A SMALL FEE. THIS PROGRAM IS VERY HELPFUL IF YOU ARE HOMEBOUND OR NOT ABLE TO COOK FOR YOURSELF. THE MEALS ARE NUTRITIONALLY BALANCED.

MOST CHURCHES OFFER VOLUNTEERS WHO ARE AVAILABLE TO VISIT AS A COMPANION, AND DO ERRANDS FOR THOSE IN NEED FOR FREE. YOU CAN CONTACT YOUR LOCAL CHURCH TO CHECK WHICH PROGRAMS ARE AVAILABLE.

PRIVATE HOME CARE COMPANIES ARE AVAILABLE TO PROVIDE CARE WHILE AT HOME. THESE SERVICES CAN VARY IN PRICE, DEPENDING ON THE LEVEL OF NURSING CARE NEEDED. YOUR PHYSICIAN AND LOCAL SENIOR CENTER CAN OFFER REFERRAL INFORMATION.

YOU WILL QUALIFY FOR HOME CARE AFTER A HOSPITALIZATION FOR EIGHT WEEKS UNDER MEDICARE PART A.

YOUR PHYSICIAN WILL NEED TO WRITE ORDERS WITH AN APPROPRIATE DIAGNOSIS, TO ENSURE THE CORRECT LEVEL OF CARE IS RECEIVED AND INSURANCE WILL COVER THE SERVICES.

THE HOSPITAL DISCHARGE PLANNING DEPARTMENT WILL COORDINATE THE HOME CARE PRIOR TO YOUR DISCHARGE, TO INSURE CONTINUITY OF CARE.

HOME CARE NURSES AND YOUR PHYSICIAN WILL MONITOR YOUR PROGRESS, AND CAN EXTEND THERAPY AND HOME CARE IF NEEDED.

UNDER MEDICARE PART A COVERAGE, SKILLED NURSING CARE MUST BE ORDERED BY YOUR PHYSICIAN, TO ALSO RECEIVE CUSTODIAL PERSONAL CARE.

ASSISTED LIVING FACILITIES ARE AVAILABLE AND ALLOW INDIVIDUALS TO LIVE INDEPENDENTLY OFFERING ASSISTANCE WITH DAILY LIVING. THESE FACILITIES CAN BE COSTLY, BUT OFFER APARTMENT LIVING, WITH THE SECURITY OF HEALTH PERSONNEL ONSITE.

CHECK THE INTERNET OR YELLOW PAGES FOR FACILITIES IN YOUR AREA.

BEST PERSONAL HEALTH PRODUCTS

INCONTINENCE PRODUCTS

ADULT INCONTINENCE PRODUCTS ARE AVAILABLE AT YOUR LOCAL PHARMACY AND MEDICAL SUPPLY STORE.

INCONTINENCE PRODUCTS ARE AVAILABLE AS DISPOSABLE
PULL UP UNDERPANTS FOR ACTIVE INDIVIDUALS, OR
DIAPERS WITH TABS FOR CLOSURE.

THE BEST ADULT DIAPERS WITH TAB CLOSURES ARE "DEPENDS WITH MAXIMUM CONTAINMENT". THESE DIAPERS PREVENT LEAKS AND ARE FOR NIGHT TIME, OR BED BOUND INDIVIDUALS. THEY ARE AVAILABLE IN SIZE SMALL, MEDIUM, LARGE, AND EXTRA LARGE.

WATERPROOF MATTRESS COVERS ARE AVAILABLE AT MEDICAL SUPPLY STORES TO PROTECT YOUR MATTRESS FROM ACCIDENTS AND SPILLS.

DISPOSABLE BED PADS ARE AVAILABLE AT YOUR LOCAL DRUG OR MEDICAL SUPPLY STORE. THESE PADS PROTECT THE SHEETS AND BED FROM ACCIDENTS AND ARE AVAILABLE IN DIFFERENT SIZES. THESE BED PADS ARE COTTON ON ONE SIDE FOR ABSORPTION, WITH PLASTIC UNDERNEATH.

LIFTING AND TRANSFERING

MOVING A LOVED ONE SHOULD BE DONE SAFELY AND WITHOUT INJURY. A GAIT BELT SECURES TO THE WAIST, AND HELPS DISTRIBUTE THE WEIGHT, TO MAKE IT EASIER TO TRANSFER FROM ONE LOCATION TO ANOTHER. STANDARD TRANSFER BELTS ARE THREE INCHES WIDE AND HAVE A LOCKING BUCKLE. THESE BELTS CAN BE UNCOMFORTABLE DUE TO THE BELT BEING THIN AND PRESSING ON THE RIBS.

THE BEST TRANSFER GAIT BELT IS A PADDED, 4 INCH WIDE 3/8 INCH THICK BELT WITH HANDLES AND INTERLOCKING BUCKLE.

THIS "SAFETY SURE" PADDED BELT CAN BE PURCHASED AT:

CAREGIVERS PRODUCTS (877) 750-0376
NORTH COAST'S FUNCTIONAL SOLUTIONS (800) 235-7054

THIS COMFORTABLE PADDED TRANSFER BELT DISTRIBUTES THE WEIGHT OF THE PERSON TO BE LIFTED, TO INSURE SAFETY, AND AVOIDS BACK INJURIES. THE SAFETY HANDLES ALLOW EASY, NON RESTRICTED MOVEMENT DURING TRANSFERRING. THE PADDING PREVENTS RIB PAIN. THE BELT IS MADE OF NYLON WITH VELOUR MATERIAL INSIDE, AND IS MACHINE WASHABLE.

MECHANICAL LIFTS ARE ALSO AVAILABLE FOR PURCHASE OR RENTAL AND WOULD NEED A PHYSICIANS ORDER. A MEDICAL SUPPLY STORE WOULD PROVIDE THE LIFT AND TRAIN YOU HOW TO USE IT SAFELY.

LOCALIZED TOPICAL PAIN RELIEF

HEMORRHOID CREAM

BEST OVER THE COUNTER HEMORRHOID CREAM IS TRONOLANE. THIS ANESTHETIC CREAM REDUCES INFLAMMATION AND ALSO RELIEVES PAIN AND ITCHING. IT IS NONGREASY, ODOR FREE AND NONSTAINING.

ASK YOUR PHARMACIST TO ORDER THIS PRODUCT IF IT IS NOT IN STOCK OR YOU CAN ORDER TRONOLANE ON THE INTERNET AT
www.drugstore.com

LOCAL ANESTHETIC

LIDOCAINE PATCHES ARE AVAILABLE BY PRECRIPTION TO RELIEVE LOCALIZED PAIN. THESE PATCHES CAN BE USED AS A LOCAL ANESTHETIC, FOR CONDITIONS SUCH AS SHINGLES. THESE ADHESIVE PATCHES CAN BE CUT TO SIZE AND WORN FOR 12 HOURS.

YOUR PHYSICIAN WILL NEED TO WRITE A PRESCRIPTION FOR A 30 DAY SUPPLY.

BEST BATHING PRODUCTS

BATH TRANSFER BENCH

BEST BATH TRANSFER CHAIR IS A SLIDING, SWIVEL BENCH DESIGN WITH HANDLES AND MOLDED SEAT.

THE INDIVIDUAL CAN SIT ON THE SEAT OUTSIDE THE TUB OR SHOWER, SWIVEL THE SEAT INTO THE BATHING AREA, LIFTING HIS/HER LEGS, AND SLIDE OVER TO BE COMPLETELY INSIDE, SITTING SAFELY ON THE CHAIR FOR BATHING.

THIS DESIGN ALLOWS TUB/SHOWER ACCESS WITHOUT EXPENSIVE BATHROOM MODIFICATION.

THIS SLIDING TRANSFER BENCH CAN BE PURCHASED AT:
U CAN STORE (866) 880-8226

MOST MEDICAL SUPPLY STORES OFFER THE STANDARD PVC BATH CHAIR, WHICH REQUIRES YOU TO SLIDE OVER YOURSELF, USING YOUR HANDS AND FEET, TO ENTER THE SHOWER OR TUB.

THIS UPGRADED SWIVEL SLIDING MODEL ALLOWS EASIER ACCESS IF YOU HAVE AN INJURY, OR NEED MOBILITY ASSISTANCE.

INFLATABLE BATH PRODUCTS

E Z TUB

E Z SHAMPOO

THESE INFLATABLE PRODUCTS ALLOW BATHING AND SHAMPOOING WHILE STAYING IN BED.

"E Z BATH" IS AN INFLATABLE FULL SIZE INFLATABLE BATH TUB.

"EZ SHAMPOO" IS AN INFLATABLE BASIN WITH NECK SUPPORT CONTOUR PILLOW.

BOTH THESE PRODUCTS COME WITH DRAINAGE HOSES FOR EASY CLEAN UP.

AN H2O BAG CAN BE PURCHASED SEPARATELY WHICH IS A PORTABLE REFILLABLE WATER SUPPLY FOR BATHING AND SHAMPOOING.
THIS BAG HANGS AND ALLOWS THE WATER TO DRAIN FROM A HOSE. YOU CAN RENT OR PURCHASE A HOSPITAL POLE WITH WHEELS, TO ACCOMMODATE THE WATER BAG.

THESE INFLATABLE PRODUCTS AND H20 BAGS ARE AVAILABLE AT:

ALLEGRO MEDICAL (800) 861-3211

HOMECARE PRODUCTS (800) 451-1903

ELDERSTORE (888) 833-8875

NORTH COAST'S FUNCTIONAL SOLUTIONS (800) 235-7054

YOUR LOCAL MEDICAL SUPPLY STORE MAY STOCK THESE ITEMS OR WOULD BE ABLE TO ORDER THEM. THE INTERNET USUALLY OFFERS BETTER PRICING, AND FREE DELIVERY.

BEST SKIN CARE PRODUCTS

INDIVIDUALS CAN PREVENT PRESSURE/BED SORES BY USING A PILLOW OR MATTRESS MADE OF EGG CRATE FOAM, GEL OR SHEEP SKIN.

GEL SEATS CAN BE USED IN WHEELCHAIRS, AND GEL MATTRESSES ARE AVAILABLE FOR PURCHASE OR CAN BE RENTED FROM YOUR LOCAL MEDICAL SUPPLY STORE.

HOSPITAL BEDS CAN ALSO BE PURCHASED OR RENTED.

YOUR PHYSICIAN WILL NEED TO WRITE A PRESCRIPTION FOR THESE PRODUCTS. INSURANCE WILL USUALLY COVER THE COST FOR DURABLE MEDICAL EQUIPMENT.

WOUND CARE

WEAR DISPOSABLE GLOVES TO AVOID INFECTION WHEN TREATING WOUNDS. TO TREAT BED SORES, CLEANSE WITH STERILE SALINE WATER, WHICH IS AVAILABLE AT YOUR LOCAL PHARMACY. COVER WOUNDS WITH STERILE SURGICAL DRESSINGS, GAUZE AND TAPE. DESITIN HELPS HEAL THE SKIN QUICKLY AND BLOCKS OUT MOISTURE. NEOSPORIN OINTMENT IS A GOOD ANTIBIOTIC TO SPEED UP THE HEALING PROCESS. ALSO USE BABY POWDER TO KEEP SKIN DRY. ALWAYS CONSULT WITH YOUR DOCTOR IF ANY WOUNDS OCCUR, TO INSURE THE PROPER CARE.

LATEX AND LATEX FREE DISPOSABLE GLOVES SHOULD BE USED TO AVOID INFECTION AND CONTAMINATION. GLOVES CAN BE PURCHASED AT YOUR LOCAL PHARMACY OR MEDICAL SUPPLY STORE.

THE BEST TAPE IS HYPOALLERGENIC SURGICAL COTTON DRESSING TAPE, WHICH COMES IN ROLLS, AND IS AVAILABLE AT YOUR LOCAL MEDICAL SUPPLY STORE.

SKIN CLEANSING

"COMFORT WIPES" ARE DISPOSABLE, PREMOISTENED WIPES WHICH PROTECT AND SOFTEN THE SKIN. THESE WIPES CAN BE FOUND IN AT YOUR LOCAL PHARMACY OR MEDICAL SUPPLY STORE.

TO DISPOSE OF DIAPERS, WIPES, WOUND DRESSINGS AND USED GLOVES, PURCHASE SMALL GARBAGE BAGS. THESE BAGS ARE AVAILABLE PLEASANTLY SCENTED.

SKIN MOISTURIZING IS VERY IMPORTANT. LUBERDERM LOTION IS HYPOALLERGENIC, NON GREASY, AND AN EXCELLENT SKIN CONDITIONER.

MANAGING MEDICATIONS

PHARMACISTS ARE ALWAYS AVAILABLE TO ANSWER QUESTIONS REGARDING YOUR MEDICATION. SOME PHARMACIES ARE OPEN 24 HOURS AND CAN ASSIST YOU DAY OR NIGHT IF YOU HAVE QUESTIONS.

PHARMACIES OFFER MEDICATION MANAGEMENT AND AUTOMATIC REFILLS. YOU CAN CHECK WITH YOUR PHARMACIST FOR DETAILS.
IF YOU SIGN UP FOR THIS SERVICE, THE PHARMACY WILL CONTACT YOU TO PICK UP YOUR REFILLS, OR THEY MAY OFFER FREE HOME DELIVERY.

KEEP A MEDICATION LOG TO MAKE SURE NOT TO SKIP OR OVER MEDICATE, AND KEEP MEDICATIONS AWAY FROM CHILDREN AND PETS. A DAILY REMINDER PILL HOLDER, CAN BE HELPFUL TO REMIND YOU TO TAKE YOUR MEDICATIONS DAILY.

PHARMACIES OFFER A POCKET SIZE PDR (PHYSICAN DESK REFERENCE GUIDE) TO CHECK YOUR MEDICATIONS FOR INTERACTIONS, ADVERSE REACTIONS AND INCLUDES DOSAGE INFORMATION.
THE POCKET SIZE PDR CAN BE PURCHASED ON THE INTERNET AT:
www.simonsays.com

BE SURE TO TELL YOUR PHYSICIAN AND PHARMACIST OF ANY ADVERSE REACTIONS YOU MAY EXPERIENCE. "THE PILL BOOK" BY BANTAM BOOKS, IS AN ILLUSTRATED GUIDE OF THE MOST PRESCRIBED DRUGS IN THE USA, AND CAN HELP IDENTIFY YOUR MEDICATIONS.

NUTRITIONAL SUPPLIMENTS

NUTRITION IS VERY IMPORTANT FOR OVERALL HEALTH. MAINTAINING A HEALTHY WEIGHT AND EATING PROPER FOODS, WILL INSURE A STRONG IMMUNE SYSTEM AND HELP AVOID ILLNESSES.

MULTIPLE VITAMIN SUPPLIMENTS ARE AVAILABLE OVER THE COUNTER. ALWAYS CHECK WITH YOUR PHYSICIAN BEFORE TAKING VITAMINS. CERTAIN VITAMIN SUPPLIMENTS CAN CAUSE DRUG INTERACTIONS.

ENSURE AND BOOST ARE NUTRITIONAL PRODUCTS WHICH CAN BE ADDED TO YOUR DIET, TO MAKE SURE YOU ARE RECEIVING THE NUTRIENTS YOU NEED TO STAY HEALTHY. THESE NUTRITIONAL PRODUCTS ARE AVAILABLE AT YOUR LOCAL PHARMACY AND GROCERY STORE, AND COME IN VARIOUS FLAVORS.

AVOIDING INFECTIONS/TAKING PRECAUTIONS

WASHING HANDS IS VERY IMPORTANT TO AVOID INFECTIONS. USE DISPOSABLE GLOVES WHEN NECESSARY, AND CLEAN SURFACES WITH DISINFECTING WIPES TO KILL GERMS.

MY PERSONAL CAREGIVING EXPERIENCE

MY CAREGIVING EXPERIENCE WAS REWARDING, AND WITH FRIENDS AND FAMILY SUPPORT, YOU CAN GET THROUGH THE MOST STRESSFUL CHALLENGING SITUATIONS.

IF YOU HAVE MADE THE DECISION TO BE A CAREGIVER, REMEMBER TO PLAN AHEAD. I HELPED MY PARENTS SELL THEIR HOME, AND ADDED AN ADDITION ON TO MY HOME. BEFORE THEY MOVED UNDER MY ROOF, I FOUND MYSELF RUNNING BACK AND FORTH ALWAYS EXHAUSTED. THE MOVE MADE IT EASIER AND LESS STRESSFUL AND I ENJOYED HAVING THEM CLOSE.

CARING FOR A LOVED ONE IS A SELF AWAKENING JOURNEY.

EVEN THOUGH IT MAY SEEM OVERWHELMING AND STRESSFUL AT TIMES, USING THIS REFERENCE GUIDE WILL MAKE IT EASIER. SUPPORT FROM FRIENDS AND FAMILY IS IMPORTANT DURING THE CAREGIVING PROCESS.

CAREGIVING FROM A DISTANCE INVOLVES A SIMPLE PHONE CALL TO CHECK ON YOUR LOVED ONE. YOUR PHONE CALL WILL REASSURE THEM, AND MAKE ALL THE DIFFERENCE.

MAKE SURE TO TAKE TIME FOR YOURSELF, TO TAKE A BREATH, UNWIND AND RELAX.

HANDLE ONE DAY AT A TIME, TO AVOID FEELING OVERWHELMED.

REACH OUT TO FRIENDS AND LOVED ONES AND ASK FOR HELP.

FAMILY MEMBERS WHO REQUIRE CAREGIVING ARE VULNERABLE, USUALLY DEPRESSED, AND EASILY FRUSTRATED. YOUR SUPPORT, PATIENCE, AND UNDERSTANDING WILL CREATE TRUST AND BRING YOU CLOSER.

www.caring.com IS A WONDERFUL WEBSITE TO ASSIST CAREGIVERS AND FAMILY MEMBERS.

I HOPE BY SHARING THIS INFORMATION, MORE INDIVIDUALS WILL BE ABLE TO BE CARED FOR AT HOME, WHERE RECOVERY IS MUCH QUICKER, AND FAMILY CAN REMAIN TOGETHER.

NOTES

INDEX

www.ingramcontent.com/pod-product-compliance
Ingram Content Group UK Ltd.
Pitfield, Milton Keynes, MK11 3LW, UK
UKHW041835200726
13854UKWH00003BA/1143

9 780557 736591